Blood Root

Also by Jessica Hiemstra

The Holy Nothing

Self Portrait without a Bicycle

Apologetic for Joy

BLOOD ROOT

Jessica Hiemstra

icehouse poetry

Edited by Sadiqa de Meijer.
Cover and page design by Julie Scriver.
Cover illustration by Jessica Hiemstra.
Printed in Canada by Imprimerie Gauvin.
10 9 8 7 6 5 4 3 2 1

Library and Archives Canada Cataloguing in Publication

Title: Blood Root / Jessica Hiemstra.
Names: Hiemstra, Jessica, 1979- author.
Description: Poems.
Identifiers: Canadiana 20240433998 | ISBN 9781773104225 (softcover)
Subjects: LCGFT: Poetry.
Classification: LCC PS8615.I363 B56 2025 | DDC C811/.6—dc23

Goose Lane Editions acknowledges the generous support of the Government of Canada, the Canada Council for the Arts, and the Government of New Brunswick.

Goose Lane Editions is located on the unceded territory of the Wəlastəkwiyik whose ancestors along with the Mi'kmaq and Peskotomuhkati Nations signed Peace and Friendship Treaties with the British Crown in the 1700s.

Goose Lane Editions
500 Beaverbrook Court, Suite 330
Fredericton, New Brunswick
CANADA E3B 5X4
gooselane.com

For roadkill

this poem's a confession
which makes you holy

My father's father's father
was a cobbler in the time of horses

I barely knew my grandaddy
who believed I was a miracle

I feel the halo of my mother's hands
easing water around my new feet

I saw an open pheasant as a child
eggs a string of pearls

the universe housed
in every dead body

I was given a stolen story
to understand who I am

what if I become
my mother

my grandmother
her grandmother

May's the month of turtles
and our highways

In the eleventh grade we dissected cats
my classmate found kittens

I couldn't smell death's sweetness
there was no blood

our cat gave birth in an old banana box
she licked each eyelid

my father drowned her litter
and I followed her mewling

she slept by the woodstove
teats swollen and hot

she searched baffled
maybe she knew

I squeezed her milk
to stop the pain

we don't need to open a cat
to understand a cat

a White man takes a bird apart
to understand a bird

a White man kills
and calls it mercy

the Dutch sang
Ere zij God, Glory to God

while slaves in Suriname
harvested sugar

for coffee after church
silver spoons in white cups

vrede op aarde
in de mensen een welbehagen

peace be on Earth
to the people whom God delights in

I've taken my father apart
to understand myself

when I don't tell the truth
it becomes vengeful

my parents lied to me
their parents lied to them

no conception
is immaculate

our world's turtles
all the way down

I inherited Jesus
whose father crucified him

I was told
this is a love story

his murder *a gift for mankind*
and also my fault

God turned Lot's wife into salt
for being homesick

mikinaak, snapping turtle
laid eggs before dinosaurs

a mother digs in gravel
I drive past her

I grew up in a church
that excommunicated people

my ancestors were farmers and blacksmiths
who got the story wrong

I don't know the names
of the people they enslaved

some sweaty nights in the city
I think even land finds me vile

I'm visited by animals in my dreams
crocodiles, foxes, beavers, whales

once I made love to a turtle
we threw ourselves over a waterfall

I learned *smite*, *excommunication*
before *orgasm*, *mudita*

in kindergarten with crayons
I drew Abraham with a knife above his son

I still fail to make sense of God
asking fathers to kill children

Dutch soldiers in Indonesia
sent a child up a tree

he tossed them coconuts
they shot him

I eat *sambal oelek*, *nasi goreng*
am told it's the food of my people

may God drown
in the rage of mothers

there's no cure
for White women

I grew up by a river in Badala
a creek in Bobcaygeon

in nations looted
by my ancestors

my parents were missionaries
so I loathe God

I think God's an asshole
to tell you the truth

I listen to snakes
they aren't the devil

I'm not ashamed of my breasts
I'm ashamed of the Dutch in Indonesia

my truck isn't horse power
soft neck of a turtle flung from her shell

I see the penis of a gelding dangling
grazing in our paddock

the diminutive for snapping turtle
mikinaakoons

Anton de Kom's mothers and fathers named bushes
parrot tongues, fiery love, hanging lamp

p'pokaitongo, fayalobi, angalampu
a firefly is *fayaworon*

a deer fly lands on me
I kill her without thinking

I don't want the truth
to be limp

I don't march
because it reminds me of church

I've failed Breonna Taylor
because I'm a coward

I still think it's about me
while the world ends

everything feels possible
when a baby's born

even love, even
a father's love

I want God
in the diminutive

I miss praying, I confess
sometimes I think I'm prayer

I pray when I hold a child
whisper to a turtle, neck exposed to crows

prayer's the bright darting
of a red-winged blackbird

I want God
to be good

my drawings are hymns
for slow ghosts of turtles

what's holy is the whole body
in light

while I'm human to be human
mothers all the way down

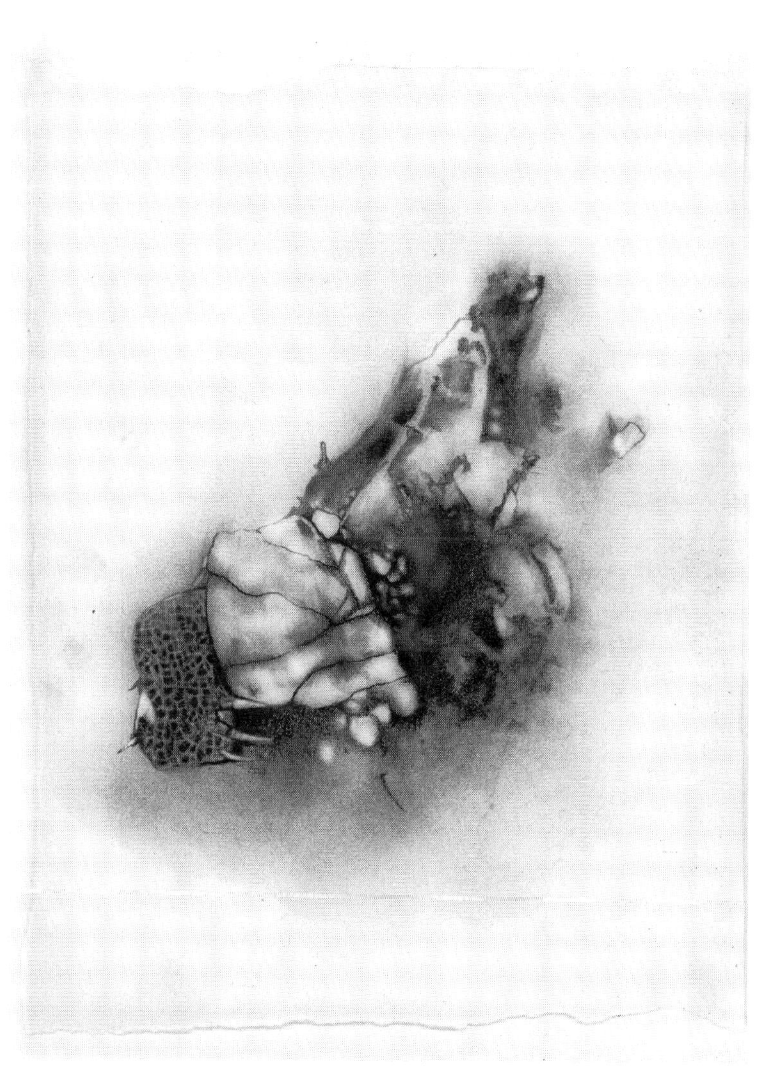

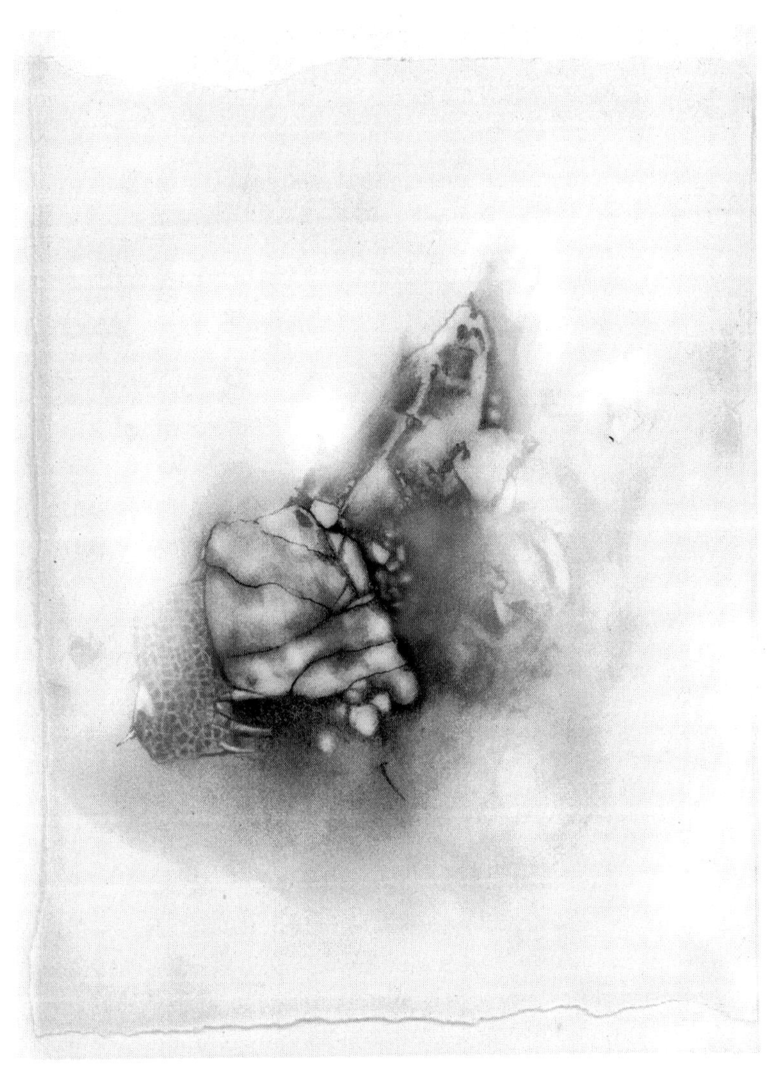

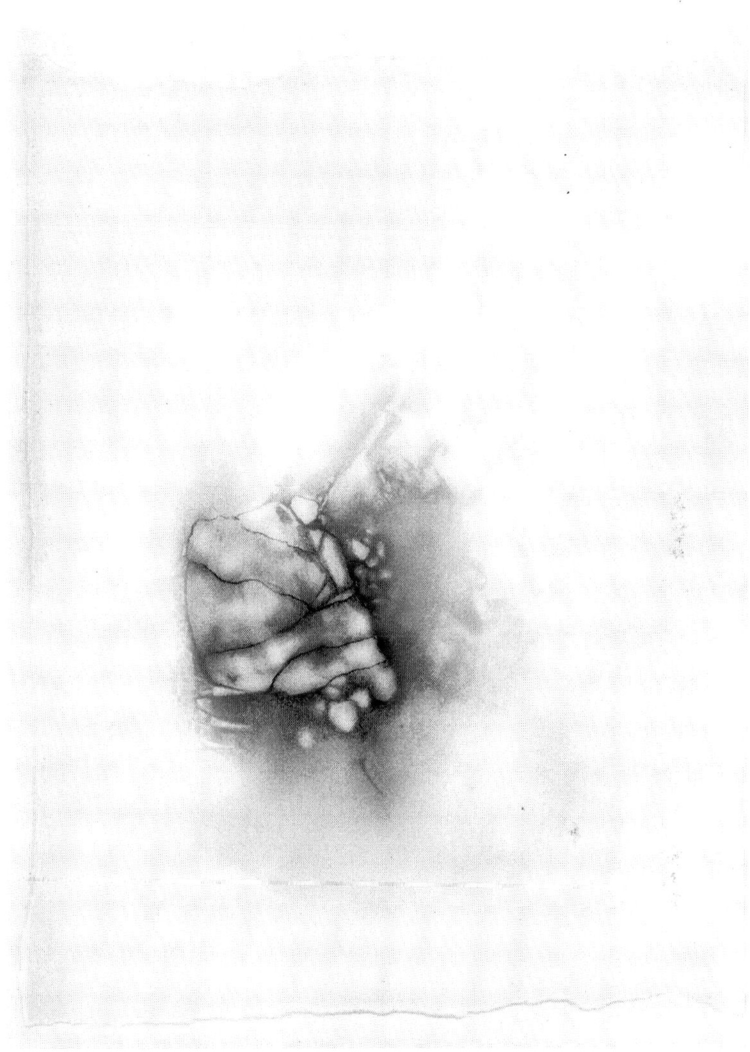

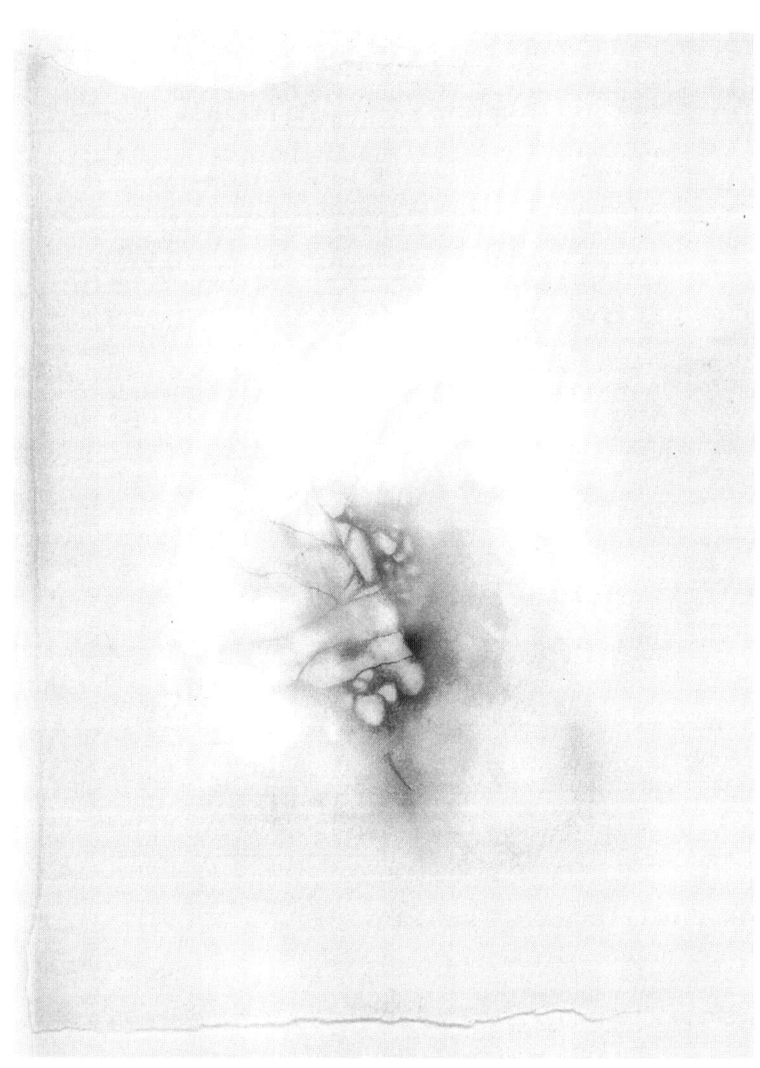

when my brother was two
he jumped into a well

I was jumping over the hole
didn't stop him when he followed me

thirty feet down
and he didn't die

this doesn't mean I can take credit
for his life

a calf sucking on my arm
close as I'll get to nursing

Mom gave birth quietly
drank advocaat after

cats eat their young
to save them from predators

I had an abortion
so no one else would bathe my child

I feel God
in the fury of men

I sing for my ancestors so loud
I drown out their answers

a cormorant dries her wings
sails above water

our hollow world flaps
red-winged blackbird bones are reeds

head down
I miss their migration

somewhere an albatross
turns to wind

something perfect and white
spills from a gull's anus

how shocking
the stillness in me

chickens of my childhood haunt me
duke claws out humping

writhing maggots in a fat white hen
panting beside the coop

I find a diary from the sixth grade

> *Bear the dog she killed another chicken this one was the sickest its stomach red with blood and it was almost dead but the poor thing was shivering to death and it was lying on its back Dad poor Dad had to kill it he has such a kind heart he never can drown the kittens when he says we need to it's kind of good because they are fun to play with*

instead, Dad waited
to kill

his gentleness
confounding mercy

bloodroot under the mailbox
closes at night

drunk with wonder
I picked a bouquet for my mother

small white hands
bright orange blood

I sit on the grey couch
fingers in my underwear

I run out of holes
ecstasy can be disappointing

a swan appears
in the moment of painful light

I think of Leda
too late to change anything

childhood's hibiscus pollen
on my nose, red beside a mango tree

dawn hunters shift past my room
gauze of mosquito net

a botanist from the Amazon
surprises me: *we don't sniff flowers it's rude*

I'm a dog in secret places
hounding private bouquets

I grew up with a screen
between my bed and cedars

sometimes I was in Badala
other times Bobcaygeon

a house with cockroaches and crocodiles
a bridge made of ropes

I doused leeches in salt, crushed them
with fragments of Canadian shield

I have no home
so I don't know who I am

a low grass roof on poles
past the blacksmith's

at the edge of town
flies on a stone statue

slick with rain and effort
hunters offered blood to ancestors

women spilled handfuls of grain
a holy place where the devil lived

I wanted to dip my finger in that blood
wipe it on my lips, communion

I'd salivate at the tinkle of glasses on a tray
white bread in neat squares

the magic of Jesus
bread like Oma's cheese sandwiches

body of Christ
on the roof of my mouth

I want to put flowers on graves
of people my ancestors brutalized

I learn Ojibwe words
for turtle

a grave can be desecrated with flowers
a childhood consecrated with duikers

I'm slung on the back of a hunter
walking home

Mom didn't know what to do with a dead bat
put it in a jar in the freezer

when letting go's too hard
we find ways to preserve the dead

bury a seed, hibiscus arrives
why can't we bury the dead like that

what we don't return to the Earth
our children inherit

language turns swimming
into two arms and an ocean

words fail the cat licking blood
from a kitten's new eyes

the villages I know aren't sanctuaries
women were raped in the forests I love

holes in trees from bullets
holes in women from rape

language can't change
what happened

if we sing at dawn wet with dew
God's the sound of a duiker dying

a thief in Badala tied to a pole
so we could spit on him

the village I remember
isn't the village now

twelve thousand years ago a girl migrated
with her family to Bobcaygeon

her family used bloodroot
for pain and insects

for the rest of my life
I'll untie a dead man

because I say nothing
I hate my mouth

I’ve seen necks slit so tenderly
I can sleep at night

a woman in Badala
cuts a hen’s throat with a small knife

tucks head under wing, gentle wheeze
slowing heart in the palm of a hand

monkeys slung on hunters’ backs
wet with holiness

forgetting how to kill
is forgetting how to sing

long car rides with goats on the roof
piss running down the window

rice fields ululate without sound
women hoeing, babies on their backs

the forest where I discovered trilliums
a graveyard because it sings still

the gurgle of blood in a dying goat's throat
communion too

I think if I eat enough dirt
I'll love the dead better

boys with slingshots in Koinadugu
peppered birds with stones to protect rice

hunters became soldiers in the war
the gods slunk out

the boys in paddies are men now
digging for gold for thieves

slick with promises
hands red with home

my great Oma
made stone soup in the war

told her children *go to bed early*
when you sleep you forget everything

Opa stole a cow
for his mother

spoke of *Dutch Nazi boys*
black shirts on street corners

when we biked to The Hague
we had our saliva ready

thin German soldiers left Holland
the Dutch refused to leave Indonesia

my people in Suriname tortured fathers
gave their children Dutch names

torture's killing someone
before they're dead

we throw blood at gods
to preserve ourselves

the moment before we die
so close to the moment after

a wing
the sound of a wing

my childhood littered with carcasses
ghosts of weaver birds in my ribs

I'm comforted by breasts
loose around our world at night

language fails
fish are fish without names

pleasure's a compass pointed home
an oyster between the legs, on the tongue

I want to hear Nina Simone
singing, *Mississippi, Goddam*

Anton de Kom's mothers
maroons naming parrots

I want to believe my grandfathers
were kind

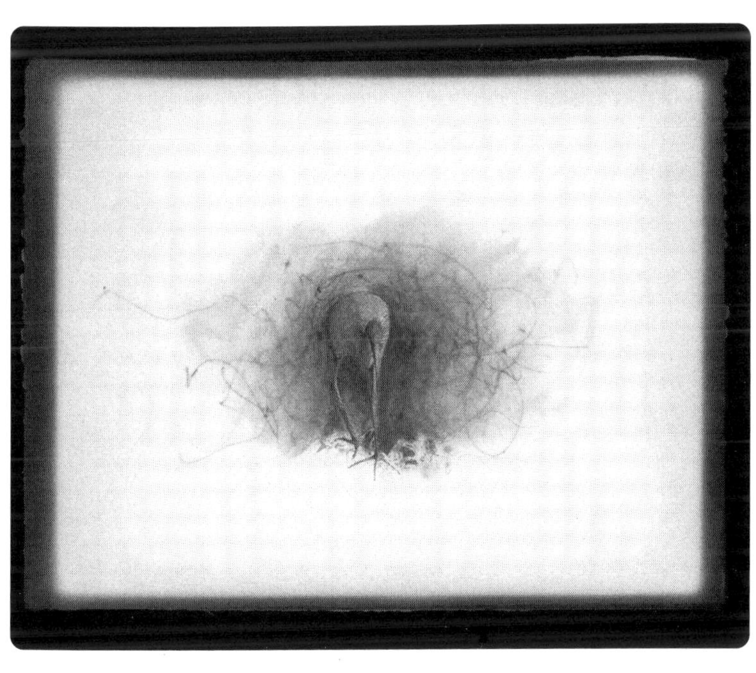

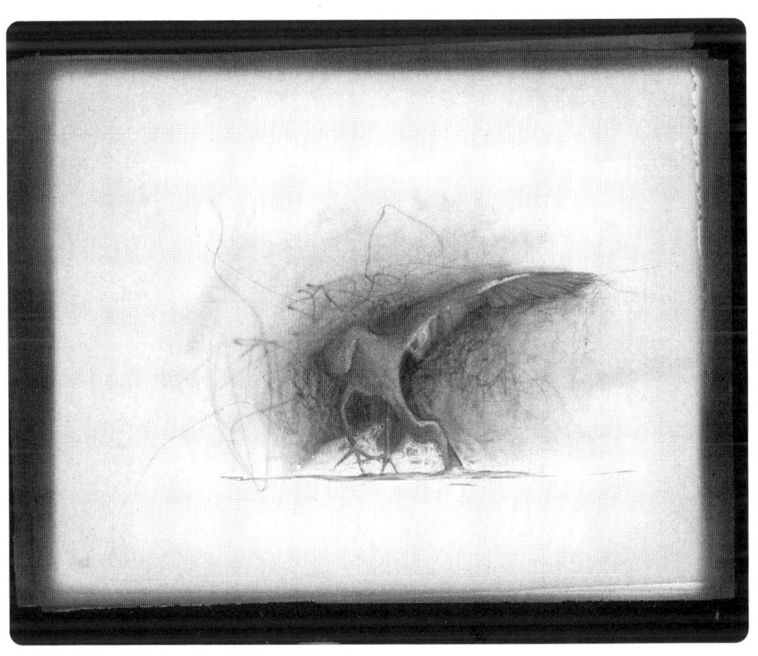

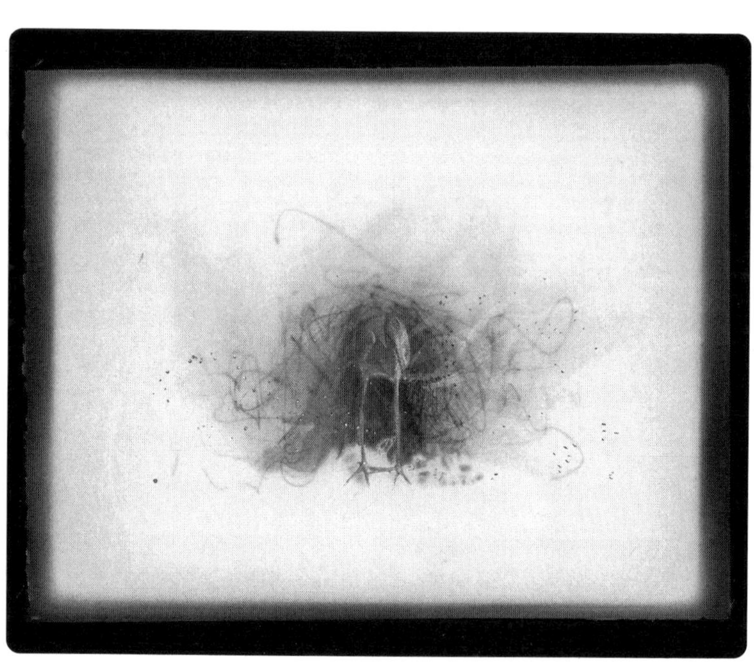

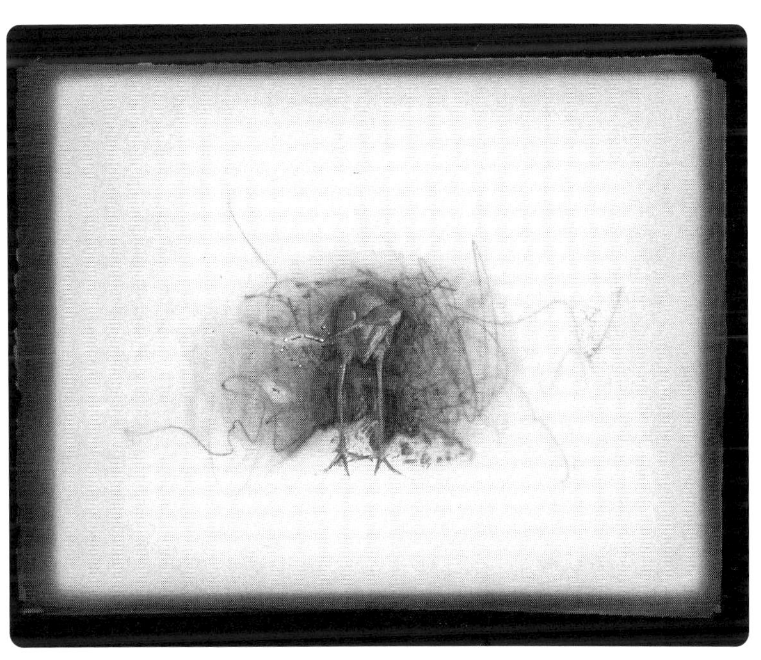

he was ferrying kola bottles
which made a magical sound exploding

he was bludgeoned by scaffolding
pinned to his seat

I walked to him
to hold his hand

soothed him like a nuthatch
the cat let go of, eye to eye, warm

I'm with you, I said
what else is there to say

to comfort a dead man
not ready to die

Oma paid a dentist to knock her teeth out
biked home with blood in her mouth

her teeth had blackened
from hunger in the war

the mystery of her bright dentures
suspended at night in water

when I couldn't sleep
she'd arrive in her nightgown

say *I love you*
no hard edges

women in bright fields plan for next year
as if it will come

Mom pulled an axe from a man's leg
as if she'd done it before

she stitched him up
with a sewing needle

crossed the Seli every day to Fiti Badala
to dress his wound

Suri the blacksmith had polio as a child
swung through Badala on two wooden blocks

I've lost the smell of groundnuts
peeled oranges, diesel, dead dog

the word for *frog* in Kuranko
but not the music

I drove to Kemptville in the dark
because I wanted wine

bellies of leaping frogs
the colour of secret parts of rice

I killed spring peepers
to get booze

being cavalier about death
is being cavalier about life

how can what we want matter
more than what we have

in Krio when you do something alone
you say *me wan kren*

me one grain
at the wheel

in Krio a *pear* is an avocado
a crocodile an *aligata*

when a boat sinks in Krio
they say *i dɔn drɔn*, it has drowned

what we call something
can't change what it is

my first memories are a hill
a farm past the statue

surprise of red ginger in the forest
August wolves, groundnuts boiled soft

language is home
an owl wing in snow

the roar of a chainsaw
is my father in the bush

when I say *father*
I don't mean you

when I say *father* your heart twangs
with a song only you know

Badala's where I learned to walk
but my feet don't belong

it's women with nets sifting silver fish
breasts sweeping, soft bells

I see those fish now
in the bellies of plovers

slippery shine in mouths
of herons, kingfishers, terns

lɛgɛ is a yellow weaver bird
djinɛ is the devil

half of Badala died in the war
thrown over a bridge into the river

the Seli became a casket
lined with alluvial gold

it's been forty years since I sang there
dwell in me O blessed spirit

devils are everywhere
especially where people drown

I can draw what I see
and it looks real

in Krio, if you've got a gift like mine
they say you *get debul*, it's *feba*, fever

a town on the Peninsula's called Devil Hole
because the devil lived there

no one's seen him in a long time
he used to wander the cliffs

my notebook smells like mildew
I draw a Maxwell's duiker, *wɔyaŋ*

small antelope with four teats
an arched back like a raccoon

February 14

I write about tides
I'm looking for the devil

I'm working for a company from Germany
that wants to end hunger through tourism

I'm divorcing the man
who scatters children from our stoop

language is never enough
our world undresses when I stand still
I've watched agama lizards all day doing push-ups
tongues flicked. I like wings at serrated edges of
mouths, a boat in an emptying channel
the shoreline's never the same
altered by how it's touched
I watch the Atlantic, startled by the swiftness
of full tide, drastic and imperceptible
I draw a starfruit, remember it in Krio
karambula, a word I knew at five
at the side of my mouth
and I can't eat it

this is before the devil takes a man
for the gold in his teeth

my notebook's a grave
I'm glad it's rotting

writing things down
cements lies

the moment I share with this man
is his death

the dog gives birth in shore stones
her puppies die, her teats must hurt

> *I watch a film of Mom on a tricycle*
> *proof how she moved as a child*
> *Manja brings me three coconuts*
> *a fat Scotsman floats in the Atlantic*
> *the Peace Corps kids so preoccupied*
> *with saving the world they don't see it*
> *dogs licking their balls*
> *a bitch's waning nipples*

I cross out bitch
everyone calls this dog Conteh

Conteh keeps me company
while my breasts shrink

I read *The Metamorphosis* on a Kindle
use the light to get to the toilet

I have diarrhea
Kafka runs to the bathroom with me

I watch *Drunken Master* movies
on the porch

> *the dog wanders*
> *nothing I know is quantifiable*

February 24

a pediatrician on the beach
tells me Gaddafi sent two pilots
into a building and they go AWOL
to spare strangers
love is possible

the Arab Spring
nothing to do with frangipani

Lebanese women put gardenias in my hair as a girl
when I didn't know this wasn't home

I can't find the story in the news
and the pediatrician's stopped swimming

I write about a boy named Ibrahim
U-turning in the current

in the mornings
I watch him paddle

in the evenings
he shares his drawings of faces

he ferries people across the channel at high tide
women with fish, mangoes, pineapples from Tokeh

all I know about tide's the moon
drawing crabs out of sand
I want to know how white birds know when to stab
angel birds, Mariatu says
cows can't see them
she says we can't see our own angels
tide's history drawing us to itself
to those we want to love
tide's regret

Ibrahim's flanking the grave
of a man about to die

Mom's ex-husband George brings me papaya
its pink flesh smells like vomit

I don't like papaya
the seeds look like rabbit shit

I'm reminded of their shrieking
Dad breaking their necks

not everyone's forgotten the war
scars carved into backs are memorials

Mankapur's son mute now
violent holes in strafed trees

I'm told sometimes someone's stabbed
when he goes to the woods to shit

reconciliation, the sister of vengeance
Fina forgives so God can punish

altala si n'hake bo a ro
God will take out my anger on him

January 6 RUF soldiers laid siege to Freetown
an anniversary marked by racists on Capitol Hill

tell me when war begins
and ends

George dives to rescue him

his head in the mouth of the river
boys searching, emergency requires
something slow in us, we can't scream
into the river or we'll choke on the devil too
we close our mouths
I hold his twenty-year-old daughter
in one motion George throws him into the boat
a sack of potatoes. No. Softer. Dough
George drags his flat hand across his throat
the man is dead it is certain
I'm standing with the dead man's daughter
with her hope and terror and tiny feet
our bodies warm, her body cut by that hand
she collapses at my feet beyond comfort
someone pries the false teeth
he's clutching to his chest, bubbles in his nose
someone gives me his teeth
I don't know what to do with them

I give her the ribbon I'm wearing on my wrist
a long inch of black silk

tie it around her wrist
this isn't your fault, I say

I thought he was waving
I thought he was waving, she says

I write like hail

we take her to her room to call her mother
her wet eyes, her small black flip-flops
her bony toes, her feet so small
Kleenex hanging out of her pocket
her head like Parkinson's, fat policemen
his purple arms, his false teeth in my hand
his sunglasses, his khaki shorts
the tenderness in her search for the room key
her voice telling her mother
Great Britain and Sierra Leone
held taut by a phone, two voices, a rubber band
Johnny enraged at the cops
for treating him like bread
never enough reverence
for the dead, even in this moment
the daughter wants little to do with me
sees my skin avoids my eyes
we two White women
disgusted by White women here
in their sandals and dresses saving children
who don't need saving
my friends push us together
like sisters
we're sisters, we're strangers
eating barracuda

George is sick for days
says the dead do that to you

when you touch them
when they aren't ready

life persists, agamas keep doing push-ups
the fishers repair nets at the same tree
Charles Taylor's defense lawyer
ordered to appear in The Hague
people stream out of Libya

liquefaction's a martini
of sand and water

River Number Two
named after two battalions

lost to quicksand
at the river mouth

frangipani blooms
Conteh leans against my chair and sighs

I'm drinking Tetley
Dad calls, tells me Gram's dead

she loved tea
loose-leaf White Exotica

her garden full of holly, a single statue
of a Black boy fishing in the goldfish pond

her birth name Ferrier
memory of horses and blacksmiths

I feel cold
I want to love her

I promise Manja not to swim in the channel
Yima says the dead man had a gold tooth

the devil's greedy for gold, she says
he should have let go

the devil wants everything
and takes just enough

I try to draw
what I feel

> *the village rises as his body leaves in the taxi*
> *how will this girl survive the flight home*
> *except by surviving the flight home*

February 27

I don't want to go into the ocean
it's not fear keeps me from swimming
but respect, water swallows everything
this isn't cleansing
the ocean's done nothing
but be an ocean

my friends beg me to stay married
selfish as telling the dead they can't go

George is robbing my mother
and I eat with him

Easter my ex-husband wants to drown
but the devil won't touch him

his head disappears into dusk
Amidu paddles out to haul him back

someone resplendent tears him a new one
for spoiling her appetite

he's furious with me
for humiliating him

the crabs at night dog nails
Conteh has fleas

we sit with our fists in the sand
he begs me to remember loving him

March 15

I love dirty handprints
on walls by beds, echoes of love
proof of contact, necessity of body
love becomes a place we inhabit
a bright blue wall, small brown lizard
evolution chooses how much regalia we need
to be wanted, a spider web on a broken bottle
a tsunami in Japan kills more than ten thousand
mostly by drowning, blunt force of sudden objects
whiff of diesel, a hand hits a wall

the dead man and his daughter
walked to the river so casually

after telling Amidu
what they wanted for dinner

I'd like to walk to my grave like that
after deciding on barracuda and french fries

March 21

I take a bus north
to where I learned to walk

at three I read the ground for hawk shadows
lifted a basket protecting chicks

wailed when they escaped
I wanted to eat them

Kuranko washes over me
I know how to greet toothless ones here

how to touch grass
without being cut

elephant grass, stick and mortar, big knife
kalɛ, kɔlɔŋ-kalaŋ, lasɛh
the village at the base of Loma Mansa
Sinikoro, under tomorrow

the flit and duck of weaver birds
my language once

I forget language
doesn't forget me

I forget this isn't home
because I feel good here

> *I wash in the night with Mankapur*
> *a bucket and the moon*
> *fall asleep to the sounds of village*
> *every noise a noise I know*
> *pots and heckling, late feet rushing*
> *with buckets at night*
> *a dog whacked by a short broom*
> *lullaby the smell of boiled cassava, plantain,*
> *dipping bats, everyone bathing*
> *spoons, radios*

my friend Marah's wife
covers bread with white cotton

the shroud of a dead man
waiting for a cab on the beach

the drip of water in a pail
grasshoppers land on fragrant pineapple

a goat cries
a child too

It's often better not to speak
this has always been my problem

the goat tied on the hill bleats
I'm a visitor in my home

Kadiatu falls asleep on my lap
I make a butterfly out of paper for her

the devil's a secret on stilts
swish of dry grass and beads

Loma people, driven east by the Kuranko
dance in crocodile masks in the forest

they left a mountain behind
Bintumani, *Loma Mansa*, Loma chief

March 30

I meet a travel writer
from the London *Times*

he knew the dead man
we are buried in our friends

he wants to know what happened
I want to know who died

he had false floorboards during Apartheid
he was a good man, he says

> *there are so many things we don't ask the living*
> *so many things we can't ask the dead*

so we ask the witnesses
who know nothing

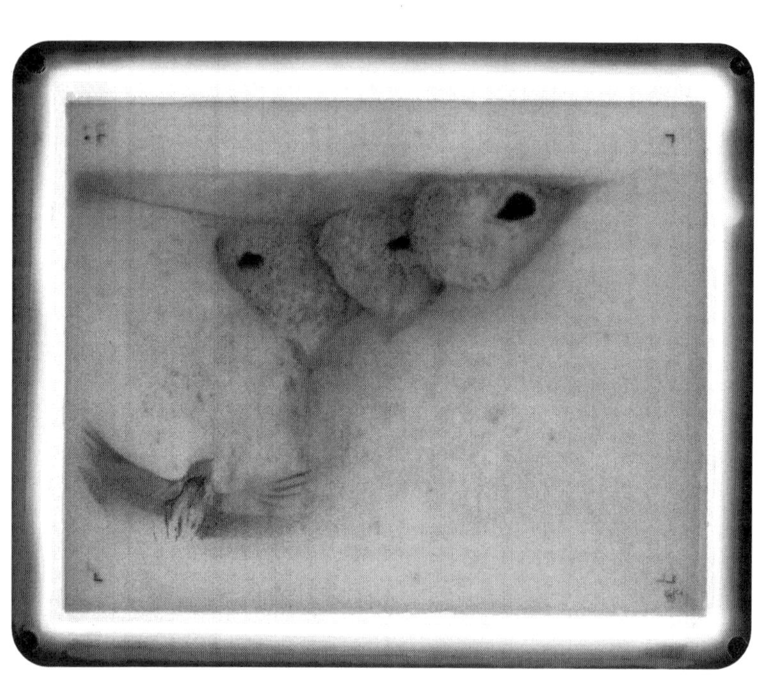

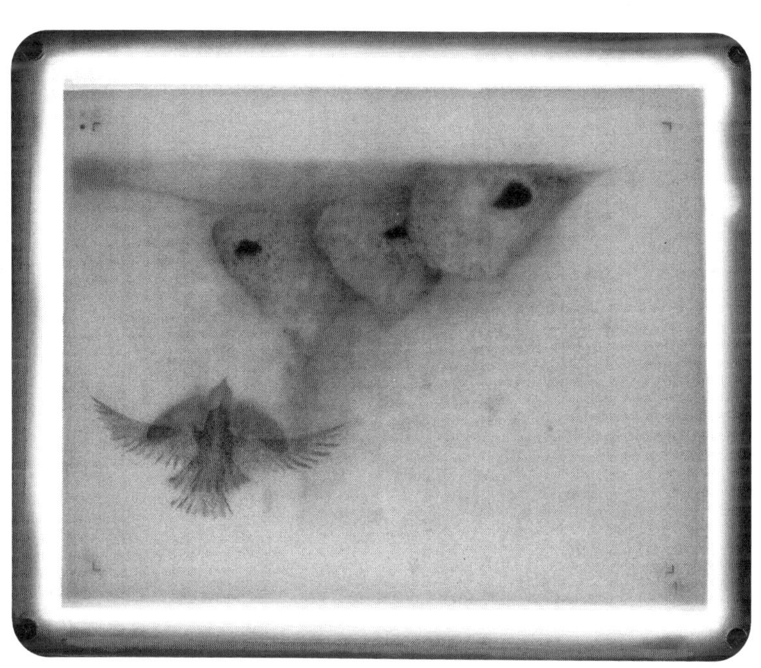

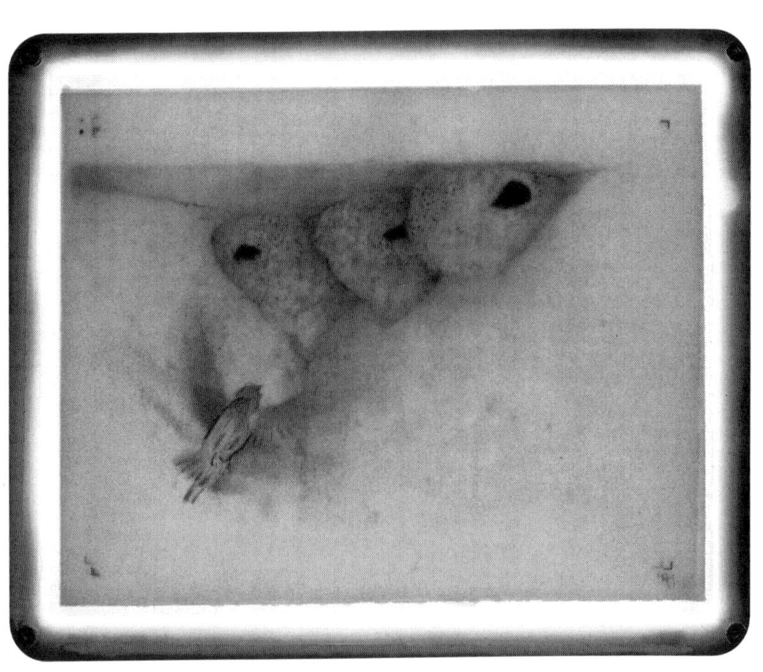

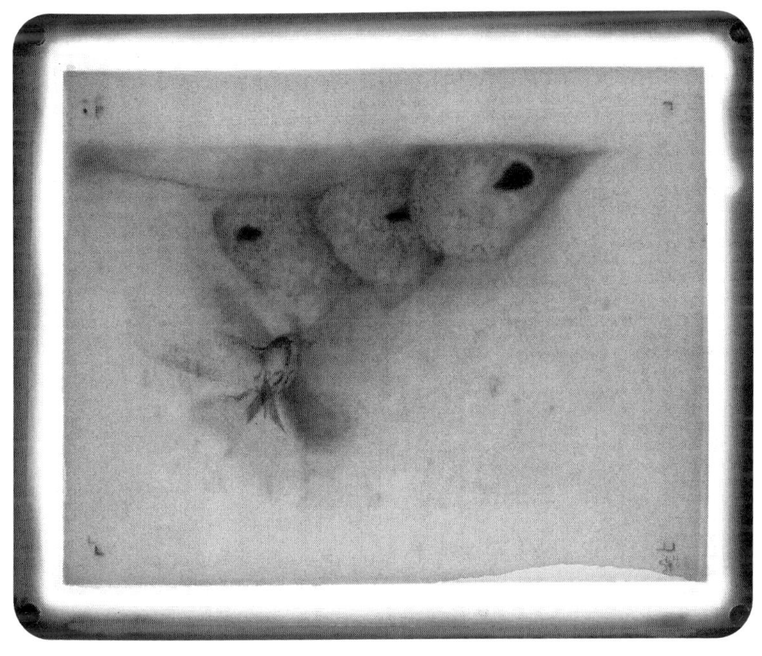

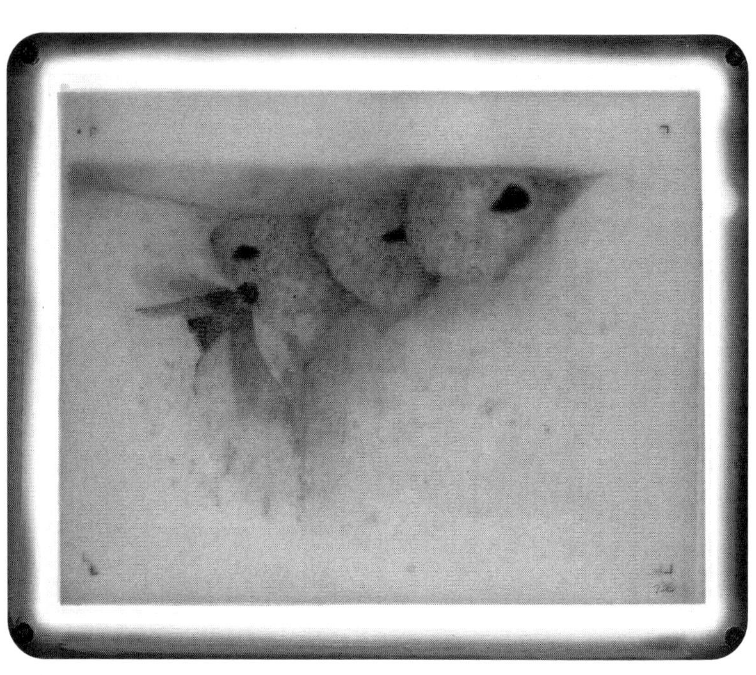

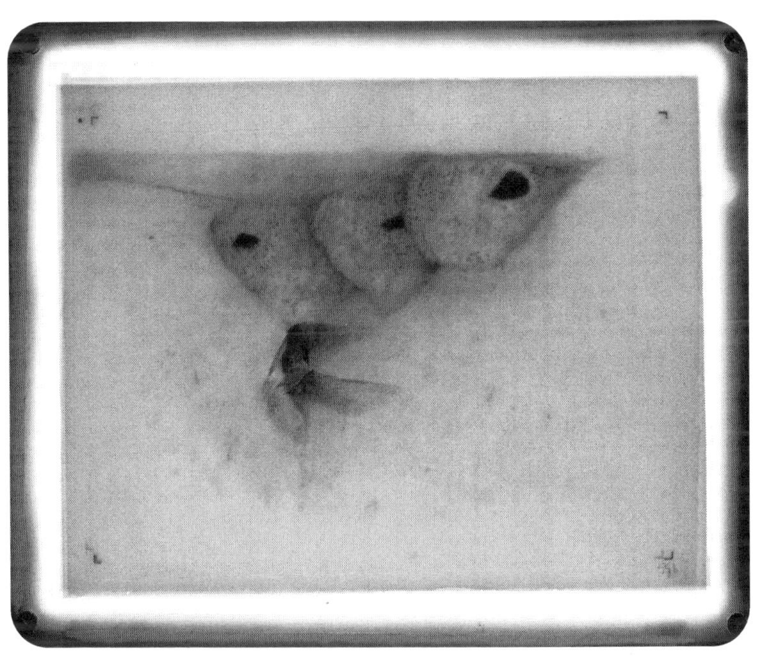

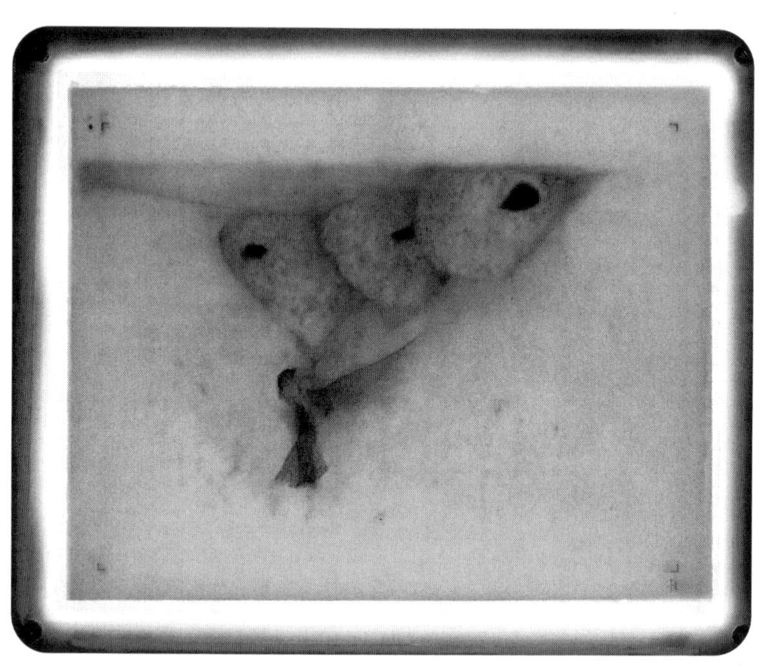

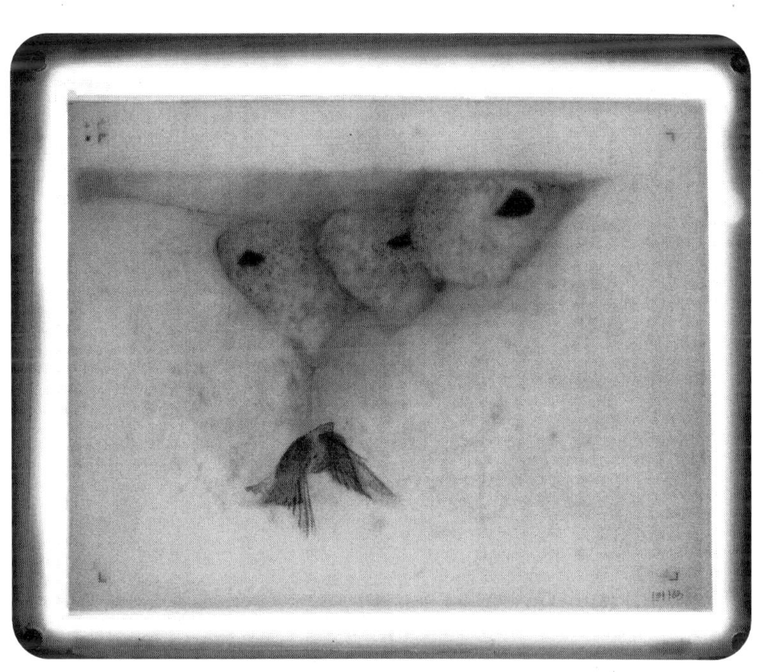

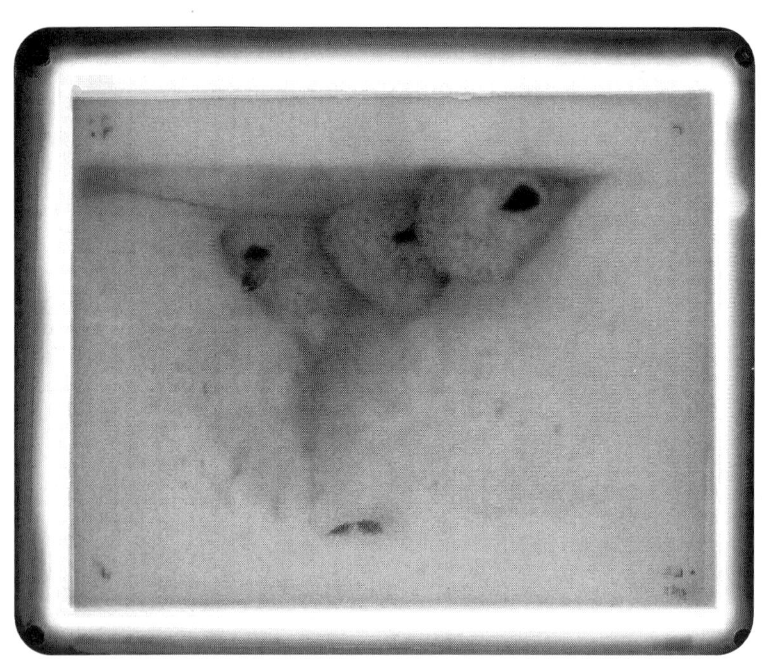

the house you grew up in
does and doesn't remember you

come out come through
this moment's a door

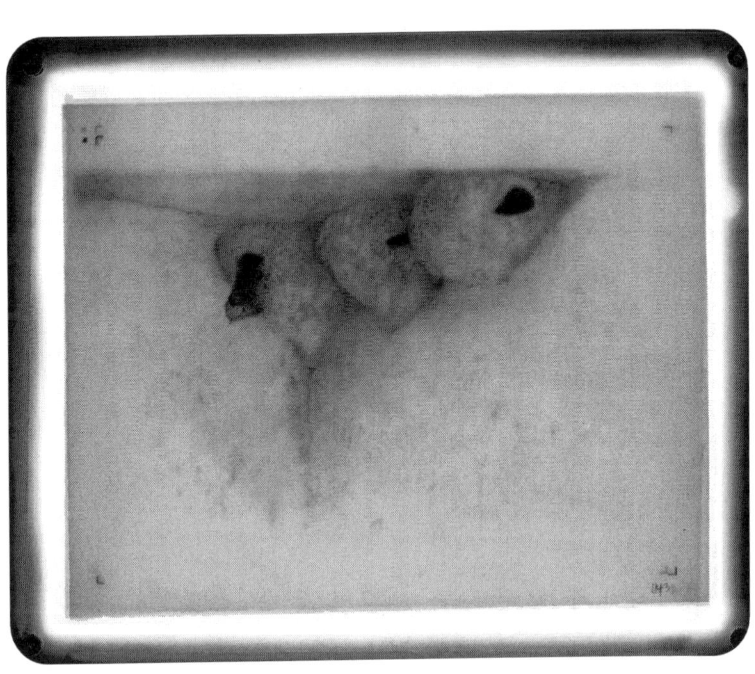

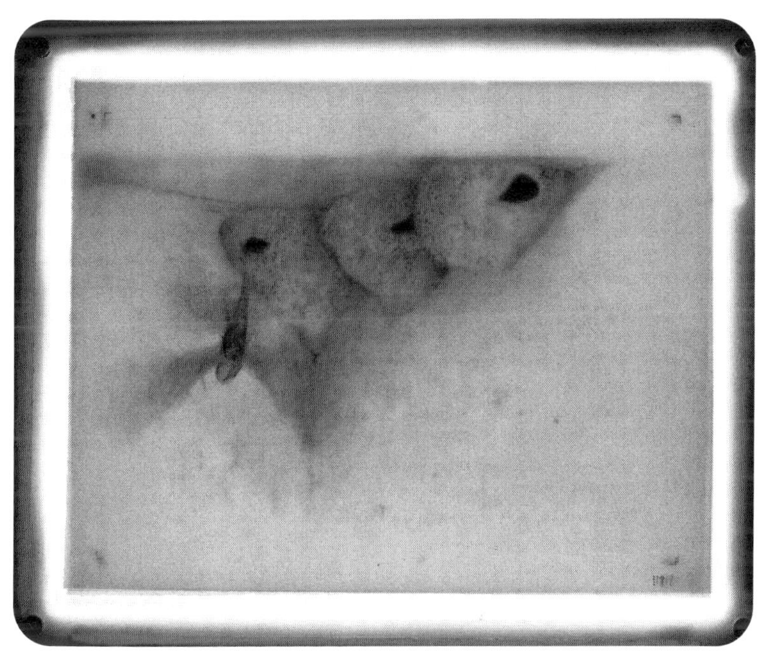

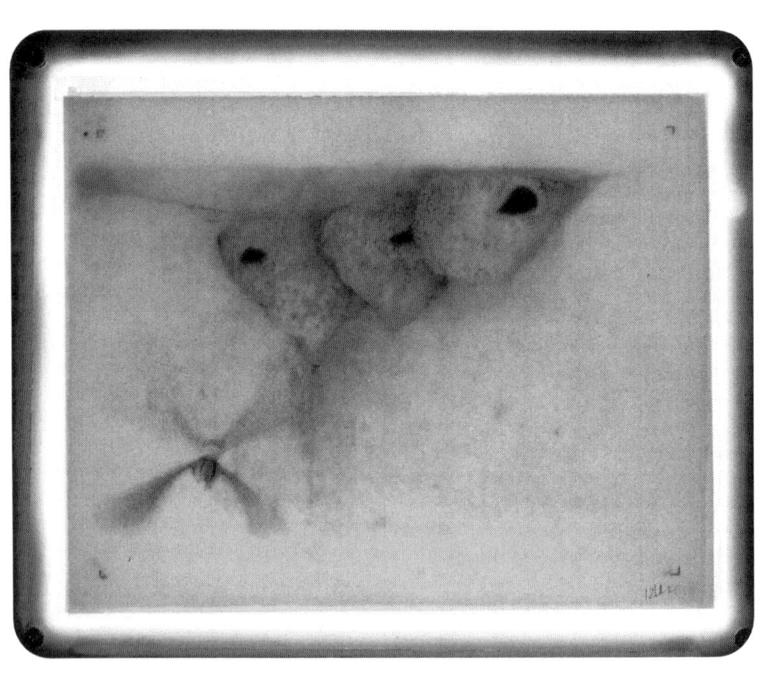

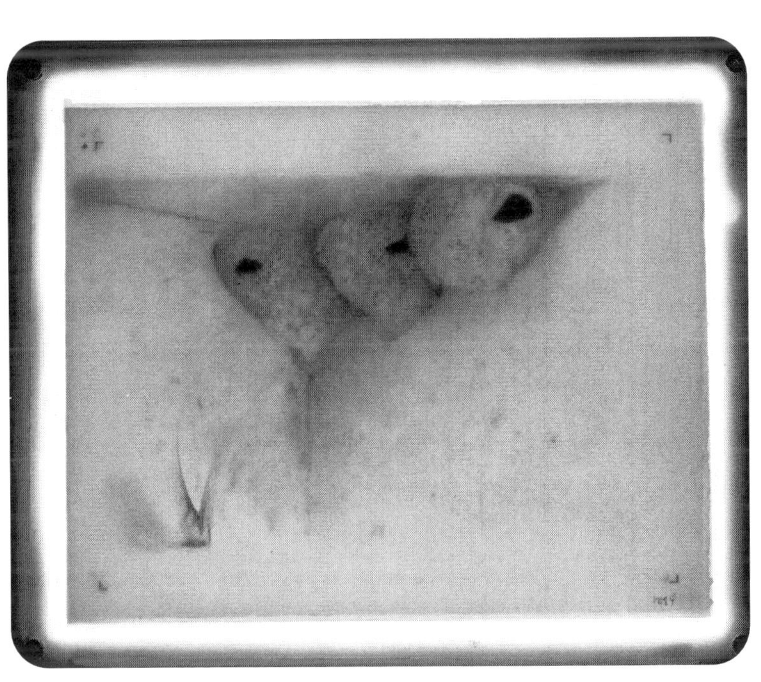

I want to land like a cormorant
when I die be remembered

like a long black neck, grace,
a small, sweet splash. I want to live

sailing through what holds me
what will we do without a sheet of ice

to love on, without your spear
in your *beautiful land* your Labrador

stain

I haven't been to your home, Nunatsiavut
Happy Valley, Goose Bay

I'm at a window in Mi'kma'ki
looking at your sculpture, *The Earth, Our Mother*

a whale bone
a song for her

someone asked you, *where are her ears*
the earth doesn't need ears, you said

it is us that needs to listen
she sees what we do

you've carved a seal
into the fin of a whale

your lines like wind and water
flight and kelp

she's *yelling and screaming*
louder and louder until we hear

mother with an angry red face
prove you love humanity, you say

our world
our exhausted mother

I dreamed a whale in Lake Ontario
the Leading Sea, *Niigaani-gichigami*

the whale was covered in lichen, groaning
air whistled through seams in her body

I woke and smelled wet dog
couldn't tell if it was me or the dream

stain

stains are memories, you said
and showed us blood on your sleeves

and stomach, told us the dark was seal
the light, fish. You put a hand on your belly

this is my blood, you said
the seal, the fish are part of me

stain

I'm the blood of people
who said *sodomy was irredeemable*

castrated men
so they'd sing better

this is one of the reasons
I want to be a cormorant

their signature of flight
waves above water

sometimes in my dreams my body's rotting
mostly in my dreams I'm home

my grandfathers beg me
God is light, says one

it's impossible to believe
you aren't a miracle, says the other

they say *it's not too late*
to learn the story

who protects
what they know nothing about, you said

I grew up singing *for the beauty of the earth*
for the glory of the skies

who can praise
what they don't tend

my ancestors split stones
with people

one day
I'll be an ancestor

Billy, you carve stone
and release dance

I'm learning
to listen to stones

stain

I walk past a man
feeding bread to mallards

it looks like communion
so I say nothing

stain

sometimes in my dreams foxes are ghosts
of people, sometimes foxes

are ghosts of foxes
sometimes I'm a fox

sometimes I'm a ghost
sometimes I'm a person

making love
to a turtle

stain

you spoke
of the seal surfacing

said you had to smash the soft part of her head
with precision, said you turned her over

put a piece of ice into your mouth
opened hers, let a droplet fall

a drink
before the next world, you said

this transforms
communion for me

stain

I'm trying to transform
into a cormorant before I die

but I'm a woman transforming
into a woman

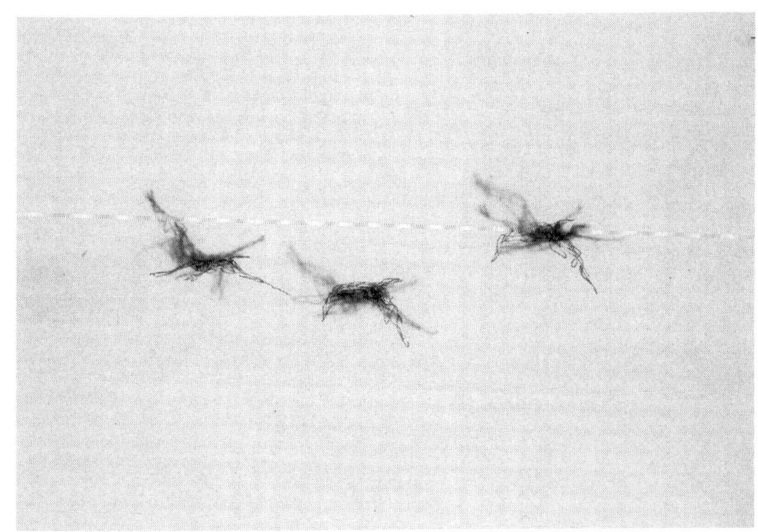

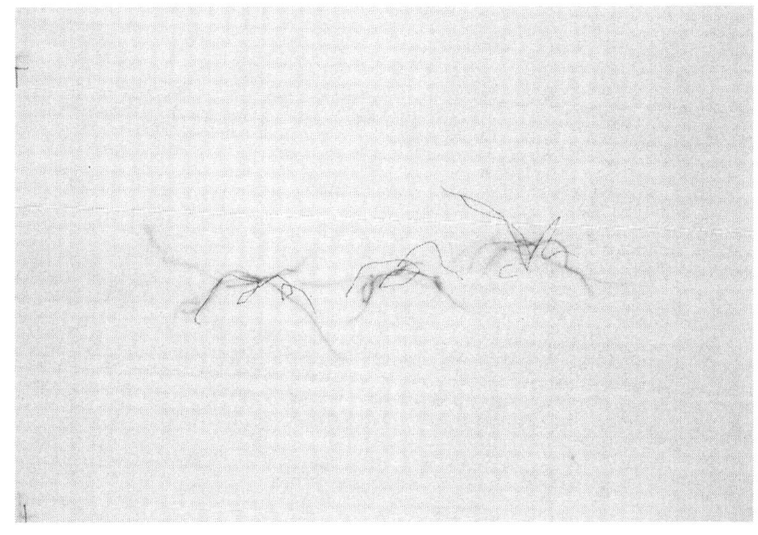

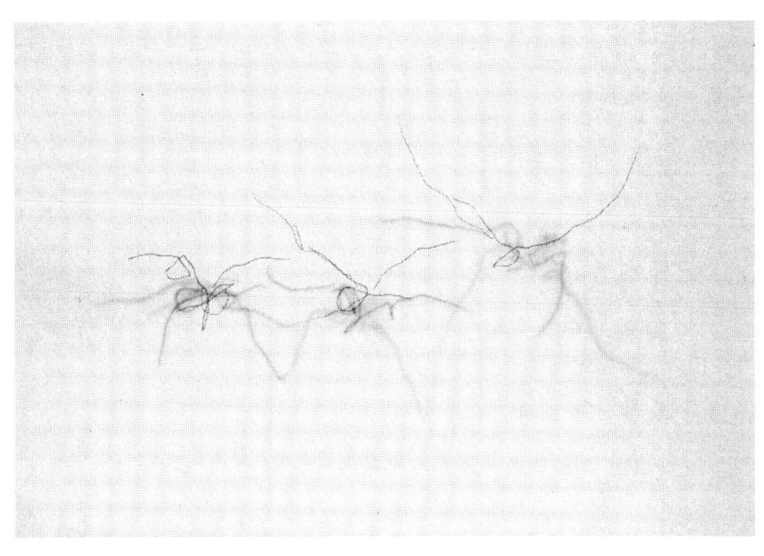

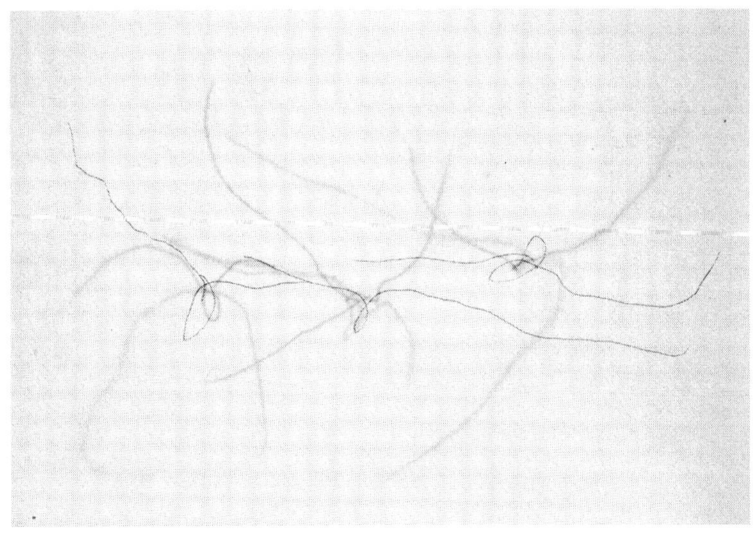

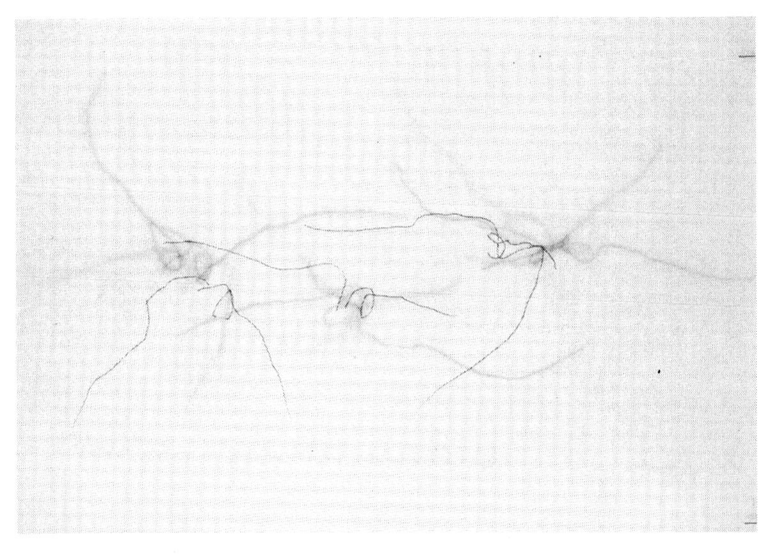

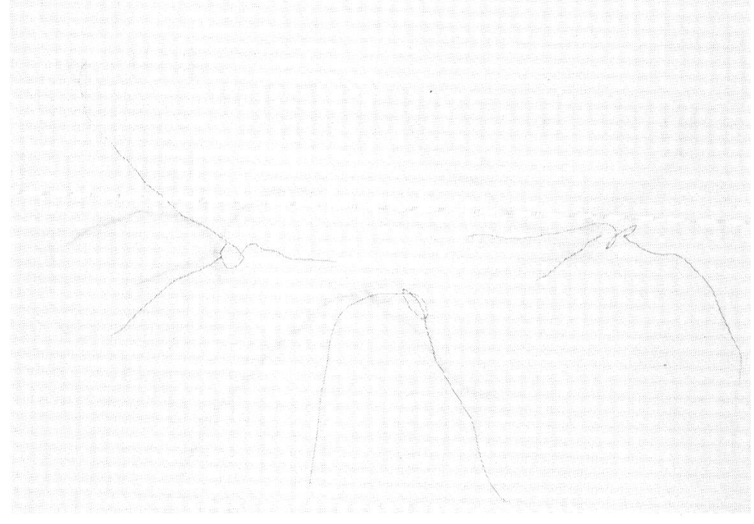

Books and places:

Pages 9 and 53: Lines in Dutch from Christian Reformed Church, *Psalter Hymnal*, (Grand Rapids, MI: CRC Publications, 1987), 214 (E Z God) and 427 (Dwell in me...).

Pages 10 and 14: The Ojibwe People's Dictionary, "turtle," accessed September 26, 2024, https://ojibwe.lib.umn.edu/search?utf8=%E2%9C%93&q=turtle&commit=Search&tyty=english.

Page 12: More about the Dutch war crimes in Indonesia can be found at https://besacenter.org/netherlands-war-crimes/.

Page 13 and following: Badala, Fiti Badala is the village of Arfaŋ Badala in Koinadugu District, Northern Sierra Leone, in West Africa. Bobcaygeon is a village in the Kawarthas in Ontario, Turtle Island. The name *Bobcaygeon* likely derives either from the Ojibwe word *baabaagwaajiwanaang* (at the very shallow currents), *giishk̨aabik̨ojiwanaang* (at the cliffed cascades), or *obaabik̨ojiwanaang* (at currented rocky narrows), or from the French *beau bocage* (beautiful, hedged farmland).

Page 15: Translations of plants and animals from Surinamese languages in Anton de Kom, *We Slaves of Suriname*, trans. David McKay (Amsterdam: Contact, 1934; Medford, MA: Polity Press, 2022), 214–15.

Page 50: The Seli River is also called the Rokel River and Pamoronkoh River. The river's waters run through the Loma Mountains, and the Guinea Highlands between the Gbengbe and Kabala Hills and the Sula Mountains in Sierra Leone, West Africa.

Page 60: Translation from the Kuranko *altala si n'hak̨e bo a ro* (God will take out my anger on him) from Michael Jackson, *In Sierra Leone* (Durham & London: Duke University Press, 2004), 68.

Page 87 and following: Quotes from Billy Gauthier taken from personal notes (2019) and an artist statement at www.therooms.ca/sites/default/files/billygauthierartiststatementreader_copy.pdf. Billy Gauthier's sculpture, *The Earth, Our Mother*, is in the Level 4 Art Gallery of The Rooms, St. John's, Ktaqmkuk, Mi'kma'ki, and is part of the gallery's permanent collection.

Thank you:

Drawings in this collection are stills from my animations. Thank you to *Palette Poetry* for publishing the animation "Cormorant," and to the Akin Vitrine Gallery for sharing the animation of the Great Blue Heron in your window on St. Clair Avenue West. Thank you, Billy Gauthier. Your sculptures and words inspired the section with stains. Your talk at the *Arctic/Amazon: Networks of Global Indigeneity* symposium at the Power Plant in Toronto in 2019 reminded me of the importance of stains, hunting, and art. I hope one day I can see your sculpture, *The Earth, Our Mother,* in person. Thank you, Aaron Kortenhoven, for helping with Krio and Kuranko translations. Thank you, Mamoud Mara, for the word for frog in Kuranko. Thank you Jonathan Taylor, poet and language teacher, for double checking my Ojibwe words. Thank you Almamy Stephen Kargo for teaching me about Badala. Sadiqa de Meijer, without your insights I would not have gone all the way. Shannon Bramer, thank you for reading an early draft and reminding me to stay soft. Kirby, thank you for believing in me and in this book. My grandparents, aunts, uncles, cousins, sister, brother, and parents—there are words in here that are hard to hold. Please know that my love and care for you is vast and unshakable. Thank you to my mother, Johanna Kuyvenhoven. Bringing us to storytellers where we lived taught me where I was and taught me to listen. Thank you to my father, Marc Hiemstra. Your belief in me lifts me. Thank you to the Indigenous caretakers of the places I've called home—the Kuranko people in Badala, Sierra Leone, and the Michi Saagiig Anishinaabe in Bobcaygeon, Ontario. Thank you, Cory Lavender, for the poetry we share.

The word for bloodroot in the Ojibwe language is *mskwiiwjiibik*

The word for frog in the Kuranko language is *tugbɔfɔrɛ*

Jessica Hiemstra is a visual artist, writer, and designer. Her writing has appeared in chapbooks, essay collections, and journals, and in three full-length poetry collections that she also illustrated: *The Holy Nothing*, *Self-Portrait without a Bicycle*, and *Apologetic for Joy*. Hiemstra won Toronto's *My Entertainment World*'s 2017 Critics' Pick Award for Outstanding Set & Costume Design for her work on Shannon Bramer's *The Hungriest Woman in the World*. "Cormorant," an animation of cormorants in flight over Lake Ontario / Niigaani-gichigami, received second place in *Palette Poetry*'s 2020 Brush and Lyre Prize for Multimedia Poetry. Some of these drawings appear in *Blood Root*. Jessica lives in Gunning Cove, Kespukwik, Mi'kma'ki.

Photo by Cory Lavender